THE CAKE COOKBOOK

RECIPES TO BAKE YOUR WAY TO SUCCESS

First published in 2012
LOVE FOOD is an imprint of Parragon Books Ltd

Parragon
Queen Street House
4 Queen Street
Bath BA1 1HE, UK

ISBN: 978-1-4454-8857-8

Printed in China

Introduction by Christine France and Angela Drake
New recipes by Angela Drake
Internal design by Jane Bozzard-Hill
Photography by Clive Streeter
Food styling by Angela Drake and Teresa Goldfinch

Notes for the Reader
This book uses both metric and imperial measurements. Follow the same units of measurement throughout; do not mix metric and imperial. All spoon measurements are level: teaspoons are assumed to be 5 ml, and tablespoons are assumed to be 15 ml. Unless otherwise stated, milk is assumed to be full fat, eggs and individual vegetables are medium, and pepper is freshly ground black pepper.

The times given are an approximate guide only. Preparation times differ according to the techniques used by different people and the cooking times may also vary from those given. Optional ingredients, variations or serving suggestions have not been included in the calculations.

Recipes using raw or very lightly cooked eggs should be avoided by infants, the elderly, pregnant women, convalescents and anyone suffering from an illness. Pregnant and breastfeeding women are advised to avoid eating peanuts and peanut products. Sufferers from nut allergies should be aware that some of the ready-made ingredients used in the recipes in this book may contain nuts. Always check the packaging before use.

contents

introduction

If you remember as a child coming home to the irresistible smells of baking wafting from the kitchen, then you'll know just how rewarding baking can be. For our grandmothers, a baking day was a weekly event in almost every home, when whole batches of traditional cakes and cookies would be lovingly prepared to feed hungry families, pack into lunchboxes or set out on pretty plates for Sunday tea.

Nowadays, many of us feel that we just don't have the time to bake cakes and since we can now buy a good variety of ready-made versions, there is no particular incentive to bake our own. But there's quite simply nothing like freshly home-baked cakes, made with love. You don't even have to spend a whole day baking to get worthwhile results – some cakes take as little as half an hour of your time. However, if you have a freezer it's often worth making a larger batch of cakes in one session as most cakes freeze successfully (without fillings or icings) and can be stored for several months.

Even if you've never baked a cake before, you'll be surprised how simple it is. All the instructions you need are given in the recipes, so if you follow the easy steps you really can't go wrong. So why not revive the baking tradition in your home - with your silicone cake pan it's never been easier!

baking with silicone

SUPER SILICONE

It's lightweight, brightly coloured, unbelievably flexible and so easy to use – silicone is the next big thing in the kitchen. This synthetic, rubber-like material can be made into a whole variety of kitchen equipment from spatulas and spoons to almost any shape or size of bakeware.

A silicone cake pan will bake a cake in exactly the same way as a metal cake tin – there's no need to change the recipe or alter the cooking temperature and the end result will be just as successful. What's more, it's a doddle to clean, takes up hardly any storage space and is virtually impossible to break!

The silicon cake pan supplied with this book can be used to make all the delicious cake recipes that follow. And when you've sampled a few of those, why not experiment with other recipes? Try home-made bread, baked or chilled cheesecakes, mousses, layered ice cream cakes or deep filled sweet and savoury pies – the list is endless!

ADVANTAGES OF SILICONE BAKEWARE

• It's heat resistant to 240°C/475°F and can be used in the oven just like any ordinary metal cake tin.

• It's durable and long lasting and won't dent, rust or buckle like metal bakeware or crack and chip like glass.

• A silicone cake pan is very lightweight and easy to store. It can be folded, rolled, crumpled or squeezed into a small space and will simply spring back to its original shape.

• It's suitable for use in the fridge, freezer and microwave so you can bake, store and reheat in the same cake pan or use it to make frozen desserts.

• The cake pan heats up quickly and bakes cakes evenly. It also cools down quickly.

• The smooth surface needs little or no greasing and cakes are easy to remove from the pan by slightly twisting or pulling the pan to release the cake then gently inverting onto a wire rack or serving plate.

• Silicone is an odourless product that will not absorb any strong cooking flavours.
• It's really easy to clean and dry and is also dishwasher proof.

HOW TO USE THE SILICONE CAKE PAN

Although silicone bakeware is considered non-stick, it's best to line the base with a circle of baking paper before use. You can also brush the sides of the pan lightly with a little sunflower oil or melted butter, if liked – this isn't essential but it will make removing the baked cake from the pan easier.

Because of its flexible nature always remember to place the cake pan on a solid baking sheet before filling with cake mixture. This makes it easy to transfer in and out of the oven without any spillages.

Don't be tempted to lift the filled cake pan by its rim as the weight of the mixture will make it dip in the centre. When the cake is cooked, lifting the pan by its rim may cause the fragile warm cake to crack across the middle.

Always use oven gloves to handle the cake pan when it comes out of the oven as it will be extremely hot. However it will cool down quickly and after about 10–15 minutes you should be able to handle it without oven gloves.

REMOVING CAKES FROM THE SILICONE CAKE PAN

To remove a warm cake, invert a wire rack across the top of the cake pan and then, holding both together (with oven gloves if necessary), turn upside down and place the wire rack on a level surface. A light sponge cake will simply drop down onto the wire rack without any help but heavier cakes will slowly slide out of the pan – you may need to pull the rim of the cake pan gently to release any suction. Flip the turned out cake with a second wire rack to position it right side up, if liked. Leave to cool completely.

A cake with a topping which may be damaged if turned upside down (such as the Blueberry Crumb Cake) should be left in the cake pan until completely cold. Remove by holding the base of the cold cake pan with both hands and gently easing and pushing the cake up and out of the pan.

CLEANING AND STORING

Before using the cake pan always check that it is clean – wash in warm soapy water and dry thoroughly with a clean tea towel or absorbent kitchen paper.

After use, wash in warm soapy water with a soft dishcloth. It can also be washed on the top shelf of a dishwasher.

If the cake pan has any baked-on marks, leave it to soak in warm soapy water for about 30 minutes then use a soft non-scratch scourer to gently rub away the marks.

With prolonged use the cake pan may have a few permanent marks that can't be washed off. Don't be tempted to scrub at them with a scourer or use a knife to scrape them away as this will damage the cake pan.

The clean cake pan can be stored with all your other kitchen bakeware. It can be folded or squashed into tight spaces but it's worth placing it in a polythene bag first as the silicone tends to attract dust particles.

DO'S AND DON'T'S

• Never use a sharp knife to slice the cake whilst it is still in the cake pan.
• Don't place the cake pan on direct heat such as a ceramic hob or expose to a naked flame.
• To freeze a cake in the cake pan, make sure both the cake and pan are completely cold before placing in the freezer.
• If you use a skewer to test if a cake is cooked through, take care not to pierce the base of the cake pan.
• When baking any recipe, always preheat the oven to the correct temperature first. Use the cooking time as a guide only as ovens can vary considerably. For fan ovens reduce the oven temperature by 10–20°C/50–70°F or follow the manufacturer's instructions.

chocolate ganache cake

SERVES 8

125 g/4 1/2 oz butter

125 g/4 1/2 oz caster sugar

3 eggs, lightly beaten

175 g/6 oz self-raising flour

1 tbsp cocoa powder

40 g/1 1/2 oz plain chocolate, melted

175 g/6 oz chocolate-flavoured cake
   covering

GANACHE

350 ml/12 fl oz double cream

280 g/10 oz plain chocolate, broken
   into pieces

PREHEAT THE OVEN to 180°C/350°F/Gas Mark 4. Place the silicone cake pan on a baking sheet and line the base of the pan with baking paper.

PLACE THE BUTTER and sugar in a large bowl and beat together until light and fluffy. Gradually add the eggs, beating well after each addition. Sift together the flour and cocoa powder. Fold into the cake mixture with the melted chocolate.

SPOON THE MIXTURE into the prepared cake pan and smooth the surface. Bake in the preheated oven for 45–55 minutes, or until risen and a skewer inserted into the centre comes out clean. Leave the cake to cool in the pan for 15–20 minutes then turn out onto a wire rack to cool completely. Cut the cake into two layers.

TO MAKE THE GANACHE, place the cream in a saucepan and bring to the boil, stirring. Add the chocolate and stir until melted. Pour into a bowl, leave to cool, then chill for 2 hours, or until set and firm. Whisk until light and fluffy.

RESERVE ONE THIRD of the ganache. Use the remaining ganache to sandwich the cake together and spread over the top and sides. Melt the cake covering and spread it over a large sheet of baking paper. Leave to cool until just set. Cut into strips a little wider than the height of the cake. Place the strips around the edge of the cake, overlapping them slightly. Pipe the reserved ganache in tear drops or shells to cover the top of the cake. Leave to chill for 1 hour.

chocolate & sour cherry cake

SERVES 8

140 g/5 oz plain chocolate, broken
  into pieces
100 g/3½ oz butter, diced
2 large eggs, separated
100 g/3½ oz dark muscovado sugar
100 g/3½ oz self-raising flour, sifted
40 g/1½ oz ground almonds
55 g/2 oz dried cherries, chopped
chocolate curls, cocoa powder and
  fresh cherries, to decorate

FROSTING

140 g/5 oz plain chocolate, broken
  into pieces
3 tbsp double cream
40 g/1½ oz unsalted butter
2 tsp rum (optional)

PREHEAT THE OVEN to 180°C/350°F/Gas Mark 4. Place the silicone cake pan on a baking sheet and line the base of the pan with baking paper.

PLACE THE CHOCOLATE and butter in a large heatproof bowl set over a saucepan of simmering water. Leave until melted. Remove from the heat and stir until smooth. Cool for 10 minutes, stirring occasionally.

PLACE THE EGG YOLKS and sugar in a large bowl and, using an electric handheld whisk, beat until pale and creamy. Add the melted chocolate and beat until thoroughly combined. Fold in the flour, ground almonds and dried cherries. In a separate bowl, whisk the egg whites until soft peaks form then gently fold into the chocolate mixture. Spoon the mixture into the prepared cake pan and smooth the surface.

BAKE IN THE PREHEATED oven for 40–45 minutes, or until risen and a skewer inserted into the centre comes out clean. Leave the cake to cool in the pan for 15–20 minutes then turn out onto a wire rack to cool completely.

TO MAKE THE FROSTING, place the chocolate, cream and butter in a heatproof bowl set over a saucepan of simmering water. Leave until melted, then remove from the heat and beat in the rum, if using. Cool for 20 minutes then chill in the refrigerator, stirring occasionally, for about 30 minutes or until thick enough to spread. Spread the frosting over the top of the cake. Decorate with chocolate curls and dust lightly with cocoa powder. Top with cherries.

classic cherry cake

SERVES 8

250 g/9 oz glacé cherries, quartered

85 g/3 oz ground almonds

200 g/7 oz plain flour

1 tsp baking powder

200 g/7 oz unsalted butter

200 g/7 oz caster sugar

3 large eggs

finely grated rind and juice of
   1 lemon

6 sugar cubes, crushed

PREHEAT THE OVEN to 180°C/350°F/Gas Mark 4. Place the silicone cake pan on a baking sheet and line the base of the pan with baking paper.

STIR TOGETHER THE CHERRIES, ground almonds and 1 tablespoon of the flour. Sift the remaining flour into a separate bowl with the baking powder. Cream together the butter and sugar until light in colour and fluffy in texture. Gradually add the eggs, beating hard with each addition, until evenly mixed.

ADD THE FLOUR MIXTURE and fold lightly and evenly into the creamed mixture with a metal spoon. Add the cherry mixture and fold in evenly. Finally, fold in the lemon rind and juice.

SPOON THE MIXTURE into the prepared cake tin and sprinkle with the crushed sugar cubes. Bake in the preheated oven for 1–1¼ hours, or until risen and a skewer inserted into the centre comes out clean.

LEAVE THE CAKE TO COOL in the pan for 15–20 minutes then turn out onto a wire rack to cool completely.

carrot cake

SERVES 8

150 g/5½ oz plain white flour

2 tsp baking powder

½ tsp ground cinnamon

¼ tsp ground ginger

150 g/5½ oz unsalted butter, softened

150 g/5½ oz light muscovado sugar

2 large eggs, lightly beaten

2 tbsp orange juice

150 g/5½ oz carrots, coarsely grated

40 g/1½ oz pecan nuts, chopped, plus extra pecan halves to decorate

FROSTING

40 g/1½ oz full-fat soft cheese

175 g/6 oz icing sugar

1 tsp finely grated orange rind

1 tsp orange juice

PREHEAT THE OVEN to 160°C/325°F/Gas Mark 3. Place the silicone cake pan on a baking sheet and line the base of the pan with baking paper.

SIFT THE FLOUR, baking powder, cinnamon and ginger into a large bowl and add the butter, muscovado sugar and eggs. Beat well until smooth, then stir in the orange juice, carrots and chopped pecan nuts.

SPOON THE MIXTURE into the prepared cake pan and smooth the surface. Bake in the preheated oven for 1 hour–1 hour 10 minutes, or until risen and a skewer inserted into the centre comes out clean. Leave the cake to cool in the pan for 15–20 minutes then turn out onto a wire rack to cool completely.

TO MAKE THE FROSTING, place all the ingredients in a bowl and beat until smooth and thick. Spread over the top of the cake and decorate with pecan halves.

blueberry crumb cake

SERVES 8

140 g/5 oz butter, softened

140 g/5 oz caster sugar

2 large eggs, lightly beaten

3 tbsp buttermilk

175 g/6 oz self-raising flour

25 g/1 oz ground almonds

115 g/4 oz blueberries

CRUMB TOPPING

55 g/2 oz self-raising flour

40 g/1½ oz butter, chilled and diced

40 g/1½ oz demerara sugar

25 g/1 oz chopped mixed nuts

PREHEAT THE OVEN to 180°C/350°F/Gas Mark 4. Place the silicone cake pan on a baking sheet and line the base of the pan with baking paper.

PLACE THE BUTTER and caster sugar in a large bowl and beat together until pale and fluffy, then gradually beat in the eggs. Stir in the buttermilk. Sift over the flour and fold in gently until thoroughly incorporated. Fold in the ground almonds.

SPOON HALF THE MIXTURE into the prepared cake pan and scatter over half the blueberries. Spoon over the remaining mixture and spread evenly. Top with the rest of the blueberries.

TO MAKE THE CRUMB TOPPING, sift the flour into a bowl, then add the butter and rub in until the mixture resembles breadcrumbs. Stir in the sugar and nuts. Sprinkle the mixture evenly over the cake.

BAKE IN THE PREHEATED OVEN for 1 hour–1 hour 10 minutes, or until risen and a skewer inserted into the centre comes out clean. Leave the cake to cool in the pan for 15–20 minutes then turn out onto a wire rack to cool completely.

spiced apple & sultana cake

SERVES 8

140 g/5 oz unsalted butter, softened

140 g/5 oz light muscovado sugar

2 large eggs, lightly beaten

140 g/5 oz self-raising flour

1 tsp ground cinnamon

$1/2$ tsp grated nutmeg

55 g/2 oz sultanas

2 tbsp milk

2 small dessert apples, peeled, cored
    and thinly sliced

2 tbsp clear honey, warmed

PREHEAT THE OVEN to 180°C/350°F/Gas Mark 4. Place the silicone cake pan on a baking sheet and line the base of the pan with baking paper.

PLACE THE BUTTER and sugar in a large bowl and beat together until light and fluffy. Gradually beat in the eggs. Sift the flour, cinnamon and nutmeg into the mixture and gently fold in using a metal spoon. Fold in the sultanas and milk.

SPOON HALF THE MIXTURE into the prepared cake pan and smooth the surface. Scatter over half the sliced apples. Spoon over the rest of the cake mixture and gently smooth the surface. Arrange the rest of the apple slices over the top.

BAKE IN THE PREHEATED OVEN for 1–1¼ hours, or until risen and a skewer inserted into the centre comes out clean. Leave the cake to cool in the pan for 15–20 minutes then turn out onto a wire rack. Brush the top with the warmed honey and leave to cool completely.

honey & almond cake

SERVES 8

75 g/2³/₄ oz butter, softened, or soft
    margarine

75 g/2³/₄ oz soft light brown sugar

2 eggs

175 g/6 oz self-raising flour

1 tsp baking powder

4 tbsp milk

2 tbsp clear honey

50 g/1³/₄ oz flaked almonds

SYRUP

225 g/8 oz honey

2 tbsp lemon juice

PREHEAT THE OVEN to 180°C/350°F/Gas Mark 4. Place the silicone cake pan on a baking sheet and line the base of the pan with baking paper.

PLACE THE BUTTER, sugar, eggs, flour, baking powder, milk and honey in a large bowl and beat well with a wooden spoon for about 1 minute, or until all of the ingredients are thoroughly combined.

SPOON THE MIXTURE into the prepared cake pan and smooth the surface. Sprinkle over the almonds. Bake in the preheated oven for 50 minutes–1 hour, or until risen and a skewer inserted into the centre comes out clean.

MEANWHILE, make the syrup. Combine the honey and lemon juice in a small saucepan and simmer over a low heat for about 5 minutes or until the syrup coats the back of a spoon.

AS SOON AS THE CAKE comes out of the oven, pour the syrup over it, letting it soak into the cake. Leave the cake to cool in the pan for 1 hour then turn out onto a wire rack to cool completely.

coconut & lime cake

SERVES 8

115 g/4 oz unsalted butter, softened

115 g/5 oz caster sugar

2 eggs, lightly beaten

115 g/4 oz self-raising flour

55 g/2 oz desiccated coconut

grated rind and juice of 1 small lime

ICING

115 g/4 oz icing sugar

grated rind and juice of $1/2$ lime

2 tbsp desiccated coconut, lightly
   toasted

PREHEAT THE OVEN to 160°C/325°F/Gas Mark 3. Place the silicone cake pan on a baking sheet and line the base of the pan with baking paper.

PLACE THE BUTTER and caster sugar in a large bowl and beat together until pale and fluffy. Gradually beat in the eggs. Sift in the flour and gently fold in using a metal spoon. Fold in the coconut, lime rind and juice.

SPOON THE MIXTURE into the prepared cake pan and smooth the surface. Bake in the preheated oven for 55 minutes–1 hour, or until risen and a skewer inserted into the centre comes out clean. Leave the cake to cool in the pan for 15–20 minutes then turn out onto a wire rack to cool completely.

TO MAKE THE ICING, sift the icing sugar into a bowl. Stir in the lime rind and juice to make a thick smooth icing, adding a few drops of water, if necessary. Spoon the icing over the top of the cake, allowing it to drizzle down the sides. Scatter the toasted desiccated coconut over the icing and leave to set.

lemon drizzle cake

SERVES 8

175 g/6 oz plain flour

1 1/2 tsp baking powder

175 g/6 oz caster sugar

3 large eggs

125 ml/4 fl oz soured cream

grated rind of 1 lemon

3 tbsp lemon juice

125 ml/4 fl oz sunflower oil

SYRUP

3 tbsp icing sugar

2 tbsp lemon juice

PREHEAT THE OVEN to 180°C/350°F/Gas Mark 4. Place the silicone cake pan on a baking sheet and line the base of the pan with baking paper.

SIFT THE FLOUR and baking powder into a large bowl and stir in the caster sugar. In a separate bowl, whisk together the eggs, soured cream, lemon rind, lemon juice and oil. Pour the egg mixture into the dry ingredients and mix well until evenly combined.

SPOON THE MIXTURE into the prepared cake pan and smooth the surface. Bake in the preheated oven for 50–60 minutes, or until risen and a skewer inserted into the centre comes out clean.

MEANWHILE, make the syrup. Mix together the icing sugar and lemon juice in a small saucepan. Stir over a low heat until just beginning to bubble and turn syrupy.

AS SOON AS THE CAKE comes out of the oven, prick the surface with a fine skewer, then brush the syrup over the top. Leave the cake to cool in the pan for 15–20 minutes then turn out onto a wire rack to cool completely.

squash & orange cake

SERVES 8

175 g/6 oz butter, softened

175 g/6 oz soft light brown sugar

3 eggs, beaten

finely grated rind and juice of
   1 orange

225 g/8 oz self-raising wholemeal
   flour

1 tsp baking powder

1 tsp ground cinnamon

225 g/8 oz prepared butternut
   squash flesh (peeled and
   deseeded weight), roughly grated

115 g/4 oz sultanas

pared orange rind, to decorate

FROSTING

225 g/8 oz soft cheese

55 g/2 oz icing sugar, sifted

PREHEAT THE OVEN to 180°C/350°F/Gas Mark 4. Place the silicone cake pan on a baking sheet and line the base of the pan with baking paper.

PLACE THE BUTTER and sugar in a large bowl and beat together until light and fluffy. Gradually beat in the eggs, beating well after each addition. Beat most of the orange rind into the mixture.

FOLD IN THE FLOUR, baking powder and cinnamon, then fold in the squash, sultanas and 2 tablespoons of the orange juice to give a fairly soft consistency. Set aside the remaining orange juice.

SPOON THE MIXTURE into the prepared cake pan and smooth the surface. Bake in the preheated oven for 1 hour–1 hour 10 minutes, or until risen and a skewer inserted into the centre comes out clean. Leave the cake to cool in the pan for 30 minutes then turn out onto a wire rack to cool completely.

TO MAKE THE FROSTING, beat together the soft cheese, icing sugar, reserved grated orange zest and 2–3 teaspoons of reserved orange juice in a bowl until smooth and creamy. Spread over the top of the cold cake and decorate with the pared orange rind.

easter simnel cake

SERVES 8

150 g/5¹/₂ oz unsalted butter,
  softened

150 g/5¹/₂ oz light muscovado sugar

2 large eggs, lightly beaten

175 g/6 oz plain flour

¹/₂ tsp baking powder

1¹/₂ tsp ground mixed spice

finely grated rind of 1 small lemon

85 g/3 oz currants

85 g/3 oz sultanas

40 g/1¹/₂ oz chopped mixed peel

550 g/1 lb 4 oz marzipan

2 tbsp apricot jam

PREHEAT THE OVEN to 150°C/300°F/Gas Mark 2. Place the silicone cake pan on a baking sheet and line the base of the pan with baking paper.

PLACE THE BUTTER and sugar in a large bowl and beat together until pale, light and fluffy. Gradually beat in the eggs. Sift together the flour, baking powder and mixed spice and fold into the creamed mixture using a metal spoon. Stir in the lemon rind, currants, sultanas and mixed peel, mixing evenly.

SPOON HALF THE MIXTURE into the prepared cake pan and smooth the surface. Roll out 200 g/7 oz of the marzipan to an 18-cm/7-inch round and place over the mixture in the cake pan. Add the remaining cake mixture and smooth level.

BAKE THE CAKE in the preheated oven for 2¼–2½ hours, or until risen and a skewer inserted into the centre comes out clean. Leave the cake to cool in the pan for 45 minutes then turn out onto a wire rack to cool completely.

BRUSH THE TOP of the cake with apricot jam. Roll out two thirds of the remaining marzipan to a round to cover the top of the cake. Use a knife to mark a lattice design in the surface and pinch the edges to decorate.

ROLL THE REMAINING MARZIPAN into eleven small balls and arrange around the edge of the cake. Place under a hot grill for 30–40 seconds to brown lightly. Cool before storing.

grasshopper cake

SERVES 8

200 ml/7 fl oz milk

2 tsp lemon juice

250 g/9 oz self-raising flour

1½ tbsp cocoa powder

¾ tsp bicarbonate of soda

85 g/3 oz butter, softened

175 g/6 oz caster sugar

2 eggs

55 g/2 oz plain chocolate, melted

25 g/1 oz milk chocolate shavings,
   to decorate

FROSTING

150 g/5½ oz unsalted butter,
   softened

175 ml/6 fl oz double cream

300 g/10½ oz icing sugar, sifted

¾ tsp peppermint extract

few drops of green food colouring

PREHEAT THE OVEN to 160°C/325°F/Gas Mark 3. Place the silicone cake pan on a baking sheet and line the base of the pan with baking paper.

POUR THE MILK into a jug and add the lemon juice. Leave for 15 minutes – in this time the milk will start to curdle. Sift the flour, cocoa powder and bicarbonate of soda into a large bowl. Add the butter, caster sugar and eggs and pour in the milk mixture. Beat with an electric handheld whisk until thoroughly combined. Whisk in the melted chocolate.

SPOON THE MIXTURE into the prepared cake pan and smooth the surface. Bake in the preheated oven for 1–1¼ hours, or until risen and a skewer inserted into the centre comes out clean. Leave the cake to cool in the pan for 15–20 minutes then turn out onto a wire rack to cool completely.

TO MAKE THE FROSTING, place the butter in a bowl and beat with an electric handheld whisk for 2–3 minutes until creamy. Beat in two thirds of the cream then gradually beat in the icing sugar. Add the rest of the cream and continue beating for 1–2 minutes until the frosting is light and fluffy. Stir in the peppermint extract and food colouring to give a pale green colour.

SLICE THE CAKE horizontally into three equal rounds. Sandwich the rounds together with half the frosting. Spread the remaining frosting over the top and sides of the cake. Decorate with the chocolate shavings.